Let's Begin WITH ABC's

QGN LEARNING

OBJECT BEGINING WITH A

Apple

Alligator

Ambulance

Axe

Airplane

Ant

Ball

Bat

OBJECT BEGINING WITH B

Boat

Broccoli

Bus

Butterfly

OBJECT BEGINING WITH

C

Camera

Corn

Candle

Chair

Clock

Crocodile

OBJECT BEGINING WITH

D

Deer

Donut

Duck

Dice

Donkey

Dolphin

Earth

Elephant

OBJECT BEGINING WITH E

Envelope

Eraser

Egg

Eagle

OBJECT BEGINING WITH F

Fish

Football

Frog

Fork

Fan

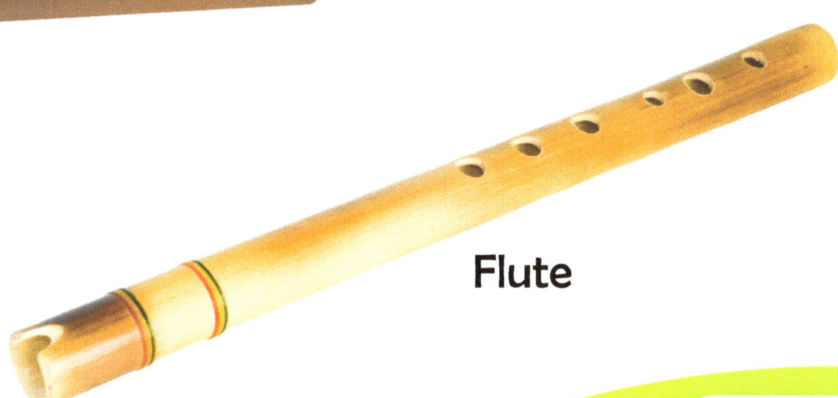

Flute

Garlic

Giraffe

OBJECT BEGINING WITH G

Globe

Grasshopper

Green-beans

Grapes

Hairbrush

Helicopter

OBJECT BEGINING WITH H

Hat

Hammer

Horse

Hippopotamus

Ice-cream

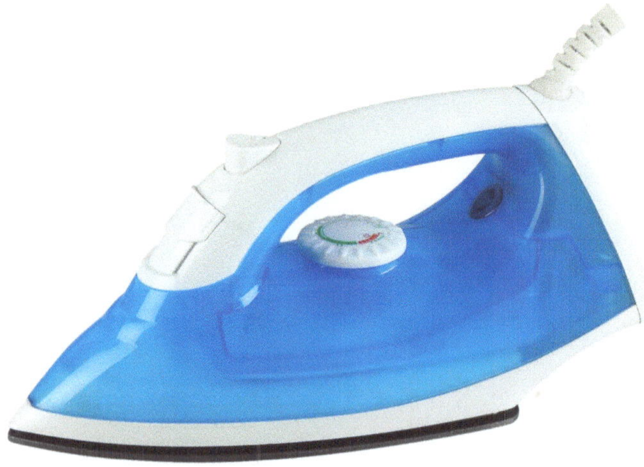

Iron

OBJECT BEGINING WITH

I

Insect

Inchworm

Igloo

Iguana

Jaguar

Jeep

OBJECT BEGINING WITH J

Jacket

Jeans

Jet

Jelly-fish

Keyboard

Knife

OBJECT BEGINING WITH K

Key

Kettle

Kingfisher

Kiwi

Lion

Lock

OBJECT BEGINING WITH L

Lemon

Ladder

Lotus

Lizard

Mango

Moon

Monkey

OBJECT BEGINING WITH M

Melon

Motorcycle

Mushroom

Nest

Nectarines

OBJECT BEGINING WITH N

Necktie

Nib

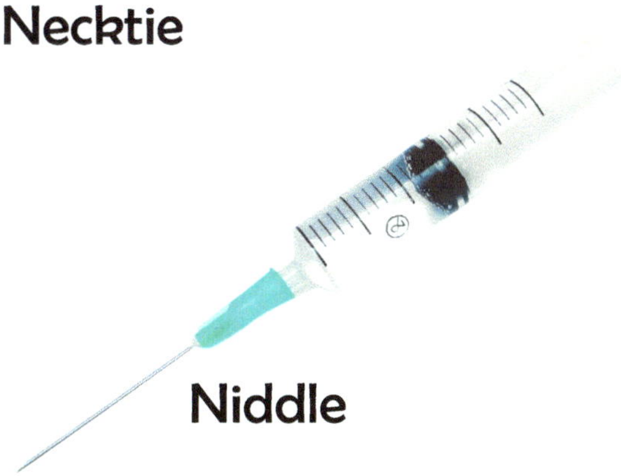

Niddle

Nut

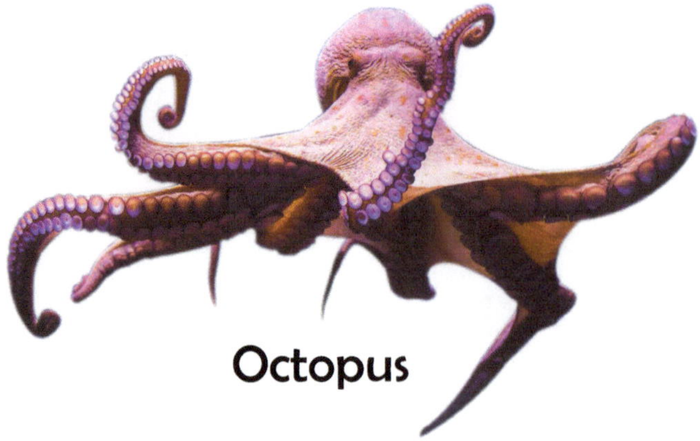
Octopus

Owl

OBJECT BEGINING WITH O

Orange

Oven

Ostrich

Onion

OBJECT BEGINING WITH

P

Panda

Parrot

Pear

Penguin

Pig

Pizza

Quill

Quail

OBJECT BEGINING WITH Q

Question Mark

Quarter Part

Quilt

Queen

Racoon

Rabbit

OBJECT BEGINING WITH R

Rose

Rope

Rat

Raindeer

OBJECT BEGINING WITH

S

Shark

Sandwich

Spider

Strawberry

Sheep

Snake

OBJECT BEGINING WITH T

Table

Telephone

Tomato

T-shirt

Tortoise

Turkey

Urchin

Utensil

OBJECT BEGINING WITH U

Urn

Unicycle

Uniform

Umbrella

OBJECT BEGINING WITH V

Volcano

Vacuum- cleaner

Volley-ball

Voilin

Vegetables

Vulture

Wallet

Walrus

OBJECT BEGINING WITH W

Watch

Wheel

Watermelon

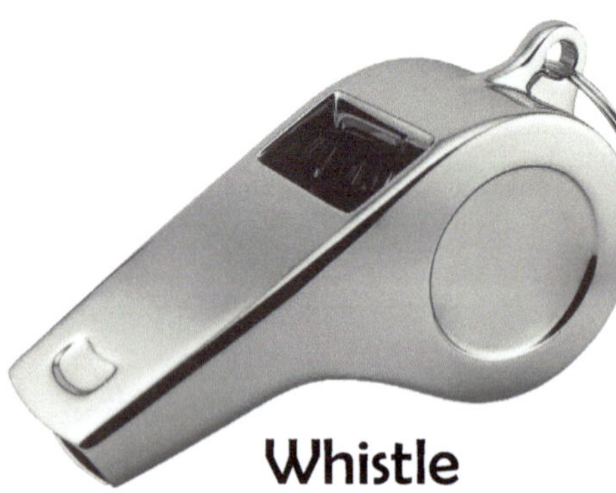

Whistle

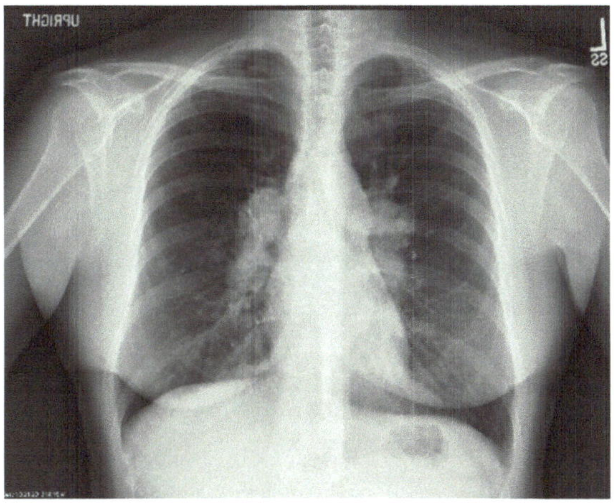

X-ray

OBJECT BEGINING WITH X

Xmas-tree

Xylophone

Xantus

OBJECT BEGINING WITH

Y

Yarn

Yak

Yatch

Yoga

OBJECT BEGINING WITH Z

Zip

Zebra

Zoo

Zuchini

REVISION

Capital alphabet letters

A B C D E F G H

I J K L M N O

P Q R S T U

V W X Y Z

Small alphabet letters

a b c d e f g h

i j k l m n o

p q r s t u

v w x y z

www.ingramcontent.com/pod-product-compliance
Lightning Source LLC
Chambersburg PA
CBHW061317170726
48282CB00021B/121
* 9 7 8 8 1 9 3 9 6 7 4 3 0 *